Living with Children

New Methods for Parents and Teachers

REVISED EDITION

Gerald R. Patterson, Ph.D.
School of Education, University of Oregon
Oregon Research Institute

M. Elizabeth Gullion, M.S.
School Psychologist, Eugene Public Schools
Eugene, Oregon

Research Press
2612 NORTH MATTIS AVENUE • CHAMPAIGN, ILLINOIS 61820

LIVING WITH CHILDREN, REVISED

Copyright © 1968, 1971 by Research Press
Seventh printing 1974

Library of Congress Catalog Card Number: 72-075090

ISBN 0-87822-000-3

Contents

Acknowledgments

The writers gratefully acknowledge the cooperation of the many families who permitted us to invade the privacy of their homes while these materials were being written.

We also wish to thank W. Sheppard, who lent his expertise in critically evaluating earlier revisions of the manuscript. The errors in presentation which remain represent behaviors which were not under the control of our colleagues' most strenuous efforts.

The writers also acknowledge an intellectual debt to B. F. Skinner, particularly for his volume *Science and Human Behavior* (1953), which stimulated much of the thinking outlined in the present textbook. Personal contacts with other investigators working on the same puzzles have undoubtedly influenced much of the thinking which is outlined in the present volume. The writers wish to particularly thank investigators such as D. Baer, S. Bijou, W. Bricker, F. Kanfer, O. Lindsley, I. Lovaas, and J. Reid for their contributions to shaping the behavior of the writers.

G. R. Patterson
M. E. Gullion

Introduction

Each year thousands of parents seek professional advice on how to handle problems with their children. It is the authors' impression that most of these problems are not caused by anything physically wrong, either with the children or the parents. In most of the families we have seen, the parents genuinely wanted to help their children. Usually they wanted very much to love their children. Very few of these parents showed serious emotional problems.

This poses a strange question. How is it that well-meaning, loving parents can have a child who behaves in a manner that makes him, his parents, and his teacher miserable?

We believe that it is quite easy for a parent to teach a child to develop problem behaviors. Also, children can actually teach parents to do some rather odd things. For example, many otherwise pleasant people find themselves "screaming" and "shouting" when they become parents.

We believe that the parent is *taught* to behave in this fashion. In the same way a child can also learn to behave in a way that irritates his parents and creates an atmosphere of conflict in the home. Our approach is one which attempts to trace, in detail, the manner in which the parent teaches the child, and the child teaches the parent.

For several years the authors of this book, and other counselors and behavioral scientists, have been working to develop a method of showing parents how to encourage desirable behavior in their children and gradually eliminate undesirable behavior. We believe it is possible to change a child's behavior without the conflict, anger and frustration that sometimes develop between parents and their children.

This method is based on a *social learning* approach. In other words, it takes advantage of the fact that people learn most of their behavior patterns from other people.

Any parent should be able to change the behavior of his or her children by using the method presented in this book. But it is important that you *use* the method—not just read about it. You should be prepared to use it over a period of time. While you may see some results almost immediately, you may have to stick with it for several weeks or months before you get all the results you want.

Before publication, a manuscript version of this book was used successfully by dozens of families. This published version includes many changes based on this experience. The authors will be interested in hearing of your experiences with this method.

How to Use This Book

This book is designed to help you understand situations in which you or your child behaves in a way that is distressing to you. The book is written in the form of programmed instruction. This is a special kind of writing that makes it easier for the reader to learn. All of the main ideas in the book have been broken down into small units or items. You are asked to *respond actively* to these items, rather than merely read them. For each of these units you will write an answer. You will be able to check each answer immediately with the one provided in the book.

This is not a test. It is a most efficient way for you to learn the main outlines of a social learning process. The questions are planned to encourage you to supply the right answer, because making correct responses helps you learn and remember.

Read each statement carefully. Write what you think belongs in the blank space in the book. The words at the bottom of each page are our suggested answers to each of the items. Use a strip of paper to cover the answers until you have written your own response. (Try not to peek at the next answer!) Then compare it with the one provided in the book. If your response is different, think about the difference in the meaning. Do not erase, but write the suggested response beneath yours. They may mean the same thing. Then continue with the next item.

SECTION I

How Parents and Children Learn

This book is about a few of the "problem" behaviors which parents have and about some problem behaviors that children have. It is hoped that the book will provide a guide for better understanding of the behavior of both parent and child. In addition to a better understanding, the material should also provide a useful basis for planning what parents can do to change these situations.

There are certainly things in the book that would be of interest to parents who do not have problem children. The general principles should be helpful in understanding ordinary child and adult behavior. For those parents who *do* have problem children, the book is intended to be used along with professional guidance. It is rather doubtful that just a parent's writing responses in this book will be all that is necessary to reshape the behavior of a problem child. However, the book can be very useful as a basis for observing and discussing these behaviors with a psychologist, school counselor, minister, case worker, psychiatrist, pediatrician, or other professional person.

1
Social Learning

1. We believe that a problem child acts the way he does,
    not because he was born that way, but because he was
    _____ to behave that way.

2. Most of what we see other people doing represents
    something they have learned. Talking, dressing, playing,
    and working at tasks are all things that are learned. It
    is also true that whining, fighting, or temper tantrums
    are _____.

3. By the time we are adults, we have learned an enormous
    number of things. We learn how to talk with our friends
    about the weather, politics, and the price of furniture

---

1. taught   2. learned

Throughout our lives, we are constantly _____ how to respond to other people.

4. People, whether they realize it or not, are teaching each other all the time. They *change* each other. Psychologists use the term "social learning" to describe the ways people te_____ or ch_____ each other.

5. Scolding and spanking are things that most parents learn to do at one time or another. It is also true that kissing, praising, and hugging are things that parents _____ to do.

6. Social learning is what we learn by associating with people. A social learning approach would suggest that if a child has been taught to misbehave, he can also be taught to_____.

7. This does not mean that a parent deliberately tried to teach a child to be bad. But many of the things parents say and do have unexpected results. Even the most well-meaning parent can _____ a child to misbehave.

8. A child is taught to steal, fight, whine, and cry. What we want to understand is HOW social behaviors such as these are _____. For example, how is it that a parent can be taught to scold and punish, or even to "love too much"?

---

3. learning

4. teach
   change

5. learn

6. behave

7. teach

8. taught or learned

2

What Are Reinforcers?

1. One of the most important things involved in this kind
    of learning is something that parents have known for
    thousands of years, but it has seldom been used very
    well. This first, simple idea involves the use of rewards
    or positive reinforcers. As we use the words here, a
    reinforcer and a _____ are about the same
    thing.

2. Giving the child a quarter as soon as he finishes mowing
    the lawn would be an example of using a _____ .

3. If you gave him a piece of cake as soon as he cleaned his
    room, the positive reinforcer in this instance would be the
    piece of _____ .

---

1. reward   2. reward or reinforcer   3. cake

4. Food and money are not the only important rewards. Other kinds of reinforcers are far more effective. One of the most powerful reinforcers for a child is the love, interest, and attention of his mother and his father. Listening to the child, hugging him, smiling at him, or talking to him are all _____, the kind that are given thousands of times *every day* to most children.

5. When you are talking, your friends reinforce you by being good listeners. In this case, their _____ is a positive reinforcer.

6. If they stopped listening to you, you would probably _____ talking or change the subject. If they did this to you very often, you would probably find new friends.

7. It is the people who provide a great deal of positive reinforcement for us that we generally choose as _____.

8. Each friend teaches you what to talk to him about. He does this by being interested in only some of the things you talk about and not in others. If you talk about something that interests him, he listens closely; otherwise he becomes bored. His listening is a powerful _____ for your talking about that particular topic.

---

4. reinforcers   5. listening   6. stop

7. friends   8. reinforcer

9. Behavior that is followed by a positive reinforcer will occur more frequently in the future. If Karl's mother praised him each time he put his toys away, it is more likely that Karl will put his _____ _____ in the future.

10. Mother's reinforcement just this *one time* does not make it certain that Karl is going to put his toys away the next time. To "really" teach him to put away the toys, his mother would have to remember to reinforce him for this action _____ times.

11. You wish your daughter would hang up her coat as soon as she takes it off. You can begin teaching her by first telling her to hang up her coat and then giving her a positive _____ when she does it.

12. There are many rewards you could use in such a situation that would strengthen the behaviors you want. For example, you could simply smile and say, "Thank you." Or you could give her a hug, or a piece of candy. All of these are positive _____ that you can use to teach your child.

13. To teach a person to respond in a desired way, we give him positive reinforcement for the desired _____.

---

9. toys away   10. many   11. reinforcer

12. reinforcers   13. response or behavior

14. If Mother reinforces both Peggy and Dad by telling them she likes or appreciates their hanging up their coats, then they both will probably _____ _____ their coats more often in the future.

15. The difficult thing is to be consistent and continue reinforcing the desired behaviors. For example, it is hard to remember to tell your child (or husband) that you appreciate his hanging up his coat. The problem is that most of us tend to take desirable behavior for granted rather than remembering to _____ it.

16. If a response isn't reinforced once in a while even after it is learned, it is likely to weaken. Positive reinforcers are necessary not only to teach a person new behaviors but also to keep the _____ he has learned.

17. Don't take good behaviors in your child for granted. Remember to _____ him once in a while.

18. When an infant cries and is picked up, he is being taught to cry. The reinforcer for his crying was _____ _____ _____.

---

14. hang up

15. reinforce or reward

16. behaviors or responses

17. reinforce or reward

18. being picked up

19. While sitting at the table, one of the children begins to laugh when the baby smears potatoes all over his face. The child then puts more potatoes on his face and also some on the child sitting next to him. Now everybody is laughing and saying how cute he is. The family is accidentally _____ the baby for being messy.

20. These examples of a baby crying and a young child smearing food are not anything that is terribly serious. They are, however, examples of how normal families accidentally teach _____ behaviors to children.

21. Sometimes it is very difficult *not* to reinforce undesirable behaviors. In the morning you are in a hurry to get Johnny to school. He can't find his clothes. He doesn't button his shirt properly. Even though he is old enough to dress himself, you are really in a hurry that morning, so you help him to get ready. In doing so, you are _____ undesirable behavior—in this case, "helplessness."

22. The reinforcer for his not dressing himself was your help and attention. If you did this many times, you would be strengthening Johnny's _____ behavior.

---

19. reinforcing   **20.** undesirable or inappropriate

21. reinforcing   **22.** helpless or dependent

23. You may have the same kind of problem when getting your family ready to go on a trip. In order to have everybody all set to leave on time, you end up doing everything for everyone. You are making it very probable that on the next trip you will have to work even _____ to get everybody ready.

24. You don't want your family to be so helpless, but you may have actually _____ them for being that way.

25. To change a situation like this one, or Johnny's, you might (for example) pick a time when you do not have a schedule to meet and announce, "Today you get dressed all by yourself. As soon as you are dressed, you can go outside (or turn on TV)." In this way, the child is being reinforced for _____ behaviors.

26. Although crying, smearing, and helplessness are not very serious, they raise the question: "How can you weaken these behaviors once they get started?" Parents frequently try spanking a child when he smears, cries, or dawdles. Spanking may work. However, there is a simpler way. In the example of the child who smeared potatoes, his family should not _____ the undesirable behavior.

27. As a second part of the same "learning" program, parents should also remember to reinforce a child's _____ table manners.

---

23. harder   24. reinforced or rewarded   25. desirable

26. reinforce or laugh at   27. desirable or good

28. If a response is never reinforced, it will be weakened. If a young child worked very hard keeping his room straight and no one ever commented or noticed his efforts, then it is very likely that this behavior would be _____.

29. If all the family stopped laughing at the baby when he smeared food, the action would eventually _____.

30. Each morning on your way to work you see an elderly man working in his garden. You say, "Good morning." He never looks up or says anything to you. After several days of this you would probably _____ speaking to him every morning.

31. Every morning Mr. Brown reads the paper while he eats breakfast. He doesn't talk while he is reading the paper. Everyone in the family learns not to talk to him at that time. He taught them this by simply not _____ them if they tried to start a conversation.

32. As most parents know, punishment is another way of weakening behavior. If you spank, slap, or threaten your child, he will stop doing whatever bothers you—at least he will stop it for a little while. Punishing and not _____ing are both ways to weaken behavior.

---

28. weakened   29. weaken or stop   30. stop

31. reinforcing, or   32. reinforcing
    answering, or
    talking to

33. However, punishment works for only a little while. A short time after a spanking, Barry can be right back teasing his little brother again. Later in the book we will outline a way of teaching your child to stop such things as teasing, without using punishment. The idea is to see to it that when Barry teases his little brother he gets no _____ for doing it.

34. Besides the fact that punishment usually works for only a short time, it also gets both the child and the parent upset. Punishment is simply not an effective way to train a child. One purpose of this book is to show a way of teaching your child that works better than

    _____.

35. So far, we have stressed two main ideas: to _____ a behavior, you must reinforce it; to weaken a behavior do not_____ it.

36. There are many things that can serve as positive reinforcers for most children. For example, listening, hugging, praise, a smile, or a kiss are all powerful rewards. Objects such as candy, and toys are also examples of _____ _____ that can be used to strengthen behavior.

---

33. reinforcement   34. punishment   35. strengthen
    or reward   reinforce or
                                         reward

36. positive reinforcers

3
How Can We Use Reinforcers?

1. For the child, *immediate* rewards are the most effective.
   The most common mistake parents make in using
   reinforcers is waiting too long after the child has acted
   before they get around to reinforcing him. To use rewards
   most effectively, the parent should reinforce a child
   _____ after he shows the desired
   behavior.

2. One mother waits five minutes to tell her son that she
   appreciated his hanging up his coat. A second parent
   reinforces her son two seconds after he hung up his coat.
   The boy most likely to hang up his coat in the future is
   the one who was reinforced after _____
   _____.

_____

1. immediately   2. two seconds

3. The second problem many parents have in using reinforcers is that they tend to take desirable behaviors for granted. Desirable behaviors should not be taken for granted, they should be _____.

4. Particularly when a child is first learning, he must be reinforced *often*. For example, when you are teaching him to wash his face, it might be wise to reinforce him *every time*. You might do this by saying, "Thank you for _____ your _____." At first, washing his face is not a duty, it is something you are teaching him.

5. In the beginning, the most effective way to teach him is to reinforce him _____ time he washes his face.

6. Also remember to reinforce him as _____ as possible after he washed it.

7. Many of the things we wish to teach a child are much more complicated than hanging up his coat or washing his face. For example, how do you teach a child to be "polite" or "to be a good student"?

    First, it is necessary to understand that "being a good student" is the last in a long series of steps. As a parent who wishes to teach your child to be a good student, it is necessary for you to figure out what these steps would be. You must also decide how you will reinforce him as he works on each of the _____ toward being a good student.

---

3. reinforced

4. washing
   face

5. every
   or each

6. soon

7. steps

8. Most complicated social behaviors can be broken down into small steps. One of the goals of this book is to teach parents how to reinforce a child as he works on each of these smaller steps. Many parents seem to want to wait until the child has climbed the whole mountain before they will get around to giving him a _____.

9. There are thousands of small steps involved in learning to be a "good child" or a "good student." When learning a new behavior the reinforcer should be given for each of the _____ steps along the way rather than as a prize at the very end.

10. Suppose the teacher says that your son Bill is not a very good student or that he is an "underachiever." What can you as a parent do about it?
    As a parent you have three problems to work out. First, how can you break the problem down into small steps? Next, how are you going to reinforce Bill as quickly as possible? Third, what kind of _____ will you use for completing each step?

11. You might begin by getting Bill to talk to you about school. Many parents make the mistake of asking their children about school and then when the child starts to tell them about it, the parent does not listen. In other words, they ask for the behavior and then they ____ _____ reinforce it when it occurs.

---

8. reinforcer   9. small or many   10. reinforcer
   or reward

11. do not

12. You might begin by setting aside ten minutes each night
    during supper when Bill is encouraged to tell about
    school. His parents or other members of the family
    must actually *listen* and *talk* to him about doing
    better work at school. Their _____ and
    their _____ to him about experiences
    at school would be powerful reinforcers for him.

13. A second step would be to get Bill to start studying at
    home. You might reinforce him on the first night if he
    could work for just ten minutes. In this situation, _____
    minutes of studying would represent a small first step
    toward the goal of being a better student.

14. It may be that Bill cannot sit still and work for ten
    minutes. In that case, it is clear that the step is too
    _____ and should be shortened to just five minutes.
    The size of the step depends on the task and the child.
    Select a beginning point that is right for your child.

15. In this way, the child is receiving reinforcement from the
    very first step of the program. As he goes along, the steps
    will become larger and he will have to do more work to
    get the same amount of reinforcement. He must work to
    obtain reinforcement, but it is your job as a parent to
    make it possible for him to be reinforced after each
    _____ along the way.

---

12. listening   13. ten   14. large or long
    talking

15. step

14

16. By the end of the first week, you might reinforce Bill only if he works fifteen or twenty minutes. At the end of such a session, you could reinforce him by asking him about the material he studied, and _____ while he talks about it.

17. Listening to him talk about his work or going over the work sheet with him would both be reinforcers. Remember that while you are reinforcing Bill, you should not criticize him or his work. Sarcastically telling him that his work is "sloppy," for instance, would not _____ the behavior of studying.

18. Teaching him to sit still and work for ten minutes is the first step, and that is all that he needs to do in order to get the reinforcement from you. A much later step might be to teach him to be neat or accurate in his work. Go one step at a time and use punishment as little as possible. If the child is trying, then _____ him for whatever step he is able to make.

19. If Bill's parents criticize or ridicule him at the first step because his work is not perfect, this will _____ the studying behavior.

---

16. listen   17. strengthen or   18. reinforce
                    reinforce

19. weaken

20. Some parents wait until their child brings his report card home and reinforce him with money or approval for getting good grades. This is not a good way to teach a young child to pay attention at school. He has to wait too long to receive the _____ and the steps he must take to earn the reinforcer are too _____.

21. Earlier we said that to strengthen a new behavior a reinforcer must be given often, and given _____ after the response.

22. Now we are also saying that to teach a child a new behavior you must reinforce him for _____ _____ step along the way to whatever goal you are working toward.

23. One reason that "bribes" do not ordinarily work in teaching children is that parents make the steps required to earn the bribes too _____.

24. Joey is told that if he "behaves" all week long, he will get a reward of one dollar. This probably will not work because he must first learn to behave for a whole hour, then a whole _____, then a whole week.

25. Let's suppose a father says to his son who is failing in school, "If you get a C in composition next month, I'll give you a dollar." It is unlikely that the reinforcer will

---

20. reinforcer or reward   21. immediately or   22. each small
    large or long   quickly

23. large or long   24. day

16

be very effective because it is too _____ a step from failure to a C for almost any child.

26. It might be better to cash in the dollar bill for 100 pennies. The pennies could be used as reinforcers, and one penny could be given for each _____ the child makes in the desired direction.

27. Different people progress at different speeds. Small steps for one person might be either too large or too _____ for another person.

28. If a child stops working, you can assume that the steps are not the right size or the reinforcer is too weak. If the child acts bored, it probably means he is not receiving enough _____ for his effort.

29. For example, suppose you decide to improve Debbie's spelling. At first you might give her a penny for spelling a three-letter word correctly. Then she must learn a five-letter word to earn a penny. Debbie is now doing more work for the same amount of _____.

30. This is a kind of "apprentice" system. When he begins, the apprentice receives his wages for very simple tasks. As he learns, he receives reinforcement (wages or praise) only for doing more _____ tasks.

---

25. large   26. step   27. small

28. reinforcement   29. reinforcement   30. difficult

31. For example, young Timmy sucks his thumb and you want to teach him to keep his thumb out of his mouth. The "steps" for this program could be increases in the amount of time that he can keep his thumb out of his mouth. The first _____ you reward might be "thumb out of mouth for five seconds."

32. During that first morning, each time Timmy is "without thumb" for five seconds you might say, "That's _____. You don't have your thumb in your mouth."

33. As your program moves along, you will notice that he sometimes leaves his thumb out of his mouth for fifteen seconds. As this happens more often, begin to reinforce him only when he has his thumb out of his mouth for fifteen seconds. In this second step, Timmy must achieve more to get the same _____.

34. Giving him a hug or a smile when you tell him how well he is doing at that time would add to the effectiveness of your _____.

35. As he moves along through these steps, you might add further reinforcement for Timmy's progress by announcing to the family at dinner that he kept his thumb out of his mouth for a whole hour that day. This would remind the family that they, too, can reinforce these behaviors. Teaching is more likely to be effective if all of the people in the family help carry out the reinforcement program. Training the child should be an affair in which the _____ family participates.

---

31. step   32. good or fine   33. reinforcement

34. reinforcement   35. whole or entire

36. Now, let's summarize the points made in this section. Behaviors that are reinforced are _____.

37. If, when the child responds, the reinforcements do not occur, then the behavior is _____.

38. When a new behavior is being taught, reinforcements should be given _____ after the behavior occurs.

39. The reinforcements should be given at first for small steps and later for _____ steps.

40. Positive reinforcers are used differently early in the training program than they are when the child already has learned the desired behavior. For example, if you were beginning to teach a child to "mind," you would try to reinforce him _____ time he minds you.

41. However, once he begins to mind you fairly well, it would then be necessary to reinforce him only every third time. Later still, he might mind you several times without your reinforcing him for it. If you forget and never reinforce him for minding, that behavior will be

_____.

---

36. strengthened   37. weakened   38. immediately

39. larger   40. every or each   41. weakened

42. Studies show that once behaviors are learned, they are more likely to last if the behavior is *not* reinforced every time. Reinforcing every time is important during the _____ stages of learning a behavior, but later on it is better if you reinforce the behavior only _____ .

43. The child who hangs up his coat regularly, even though his mother reinforces him for it only occasionally, is more likely to have a long-lasting habit than the child whose mother reinforces him _____ time he hangs up his coat.

---

42. early
occasionally

43. every

4

Social and Non-Social Reinforcers

1. Awarding food, money, love, or attention for behavior is positive reinforcement. A mother listening to her child is giving him a _____ reinforcer.

2. Food, money, candy, and toys are non-social reinforcers. Praise, smiles, approval, attention, and kisses are examples of social reinforcers. A pat on the back would be a _____ reinforcer.

3. Staring out the window as your husband talks to you would not be a reinforcer for his talking. Smiling or laughing at the clever things he says could be a powerful s_____ r_____ .

---

1. positive   2. social   3. social reinforcer

4. Both adults and children receive thousands of these social reinforcers each day, but most people do not notice what it is that other people reinforce us for. Also, the changes in behavior are so slow we don't notice they are happening. Most behaviors are learned as a result of _____ _____.

5. Social reinforcers are "small" events that happen to a child thousands of times each day. Slowly, as a result of these events, the child acquires a "personality." Unless you learn to observe what it is that a child is being reinforced *for*, you will probably not understand how the child _____ that personality.

6. All the programs used for changing some undesirable child behaviors stress the importance of social reinforcers given by the parent. Often, however, the first steps in the beginning of these programs stress non-_____ reinforcers, such as money, candy, toys, or "points."

7. The reason for this is that the relationship between many parents and their children has been so unpleasant for so long that at first social reinforcers from the parents just do not work very well. During the first few steps, when the child is again learning to respond to his parents, it is often wise to use both _____ and _____ reinforcers.

---

4. social reinforcement   **5.** learned or developed

6. social   **7.** social
                            non-social

8. Another kind of non-social reinforcer that has worked well is the "point system." In this method, the child earns points (which mother or child writes down). Later, the child trades in his points for money, toys, or something important to him. Earning 500 _____ for a fishing trip might be a goal in a boy's point system.

9. The parents and a younger child might decide that when he has earned 100 points he can buy a model airplane. In this system, each point is a _____.

10. The child receives a point immediately following the desired behavior. For example, when he washes his face, his mother _____ records the point in his notebook.

11. Tell your child when you make such a mark. You might say, "That was good. I'll mark another _____ in your book."

12. At the end of the day, tell him how many points he has earned. Set up a contract with him so that he knows what he is earning with the _____.

13. In this program you are using both social and non-social _____ to strengthen self helping behavior.

---

8. points   9. reinforcer   10. immediately

11. point   12. points   13. reinforcers

14. The first few days, points may be worth a penny each. Later, it may take three or four to earn one _____.

15. This procedure can be rather flexible because parents and child can change the system from one week to the next. One week he may be earning pennies, another week he may be earning points to go on a trip with his father. What the points will earn is up to the _____ and the child. In this way, a good retraining program is tailor-made for the individual child and his family.

---

14. penny   15. parents

5

Children Train Parents

1. There is more to life than just positive reinforcers. There are things that happen in the life of adults and children that are painful. For example, electric shock, being pinched or bumped hard, being burned, being near a very loud noise, being yelled at or spanked. For most children, being scolded would be a _____ event.

2. A child runs through the house yelling and shouting. Mother is very tired and has a headache. She is lying down and trying to get some rest. Very likely, the child's yelling and screaming is _____ to her.

---

1. painful   2. painful

3. Anything that will "turn off" a painful event is strengthened. Behaviors that turn off painful events are
_____.

4. Most of us learn to avoid or get away from _____
_____.

5. Some things parents do to their children were learned and strengthened because they helped turn off painful events. For example, Mr. Harvey comes home tired. The children are being loud and noisy. He sits down and turns on the TV set, and then he can't hear the yelling any more. The behavior "turn on the TV" was _____.

6. A response that is reinforced is more likely to occur again in the future. If a response is successful in turning off a painful event, that response will occur _____ frequently in the future.

7. That means that next time Mr. Harvey comes home tired out and the children are being very noisy, the thing he is likely to do is to _____ ____ _____ _____.

---

3. strengthened or reinforced

4. painful events

5. learned or strengthened

6. more

7. turn on the TV

8. Another thing the tired father might have done was to shout, "Shut up," and threaten to slap the next noise maker. Often this works, and for a short time the children stop making noise. In this case, the children are _____ their father for shouting and threatening.

9. Next time the children make noise, the thing that this father is most likely to do is to yell _____ ____.

10. If this happened a number of times, the children would actually train the _____ ; but probably neither the father or the children would be aware of this fact. Mr. Harvey may be thinking, "That'll teach those kids not to be so noisy!" But who is teaching whom?

11. Mrs. Moore is loud and bossy; she is nagging morning and evening. She seldom has a pleasant thing to say to anyone. Her husband manages to disappear every night—bowling, working, or going to meetings. For him, getting out of the home at night is strengthened because it turns off his wife's nagging. Mrs. Moore has _____ her husband to stay away from home.

12. The painful event being avoided in this kind of training would be the _____.

---

8. reinforcing   9. "Shut up"   10. father

11. trained or taught   12. nagging

13. The behavior that is reinforced because it turns off the nagging would be _____ .

14. Mrs. Moore is accidentally providing _____ that result in her husband's learning to leave the house.

15. A behavior that helps you *avoid* something unpleasant is strengthened. For example, *not* going to the dentist's for a checkup is reinforced because it makes it possible for you to _____ an unpleasant situation.

16. Aunt Minnie complains all the time. Each time you see her she has new aches or at least a new medicine. She has few interests other than what is wrong with her own body. As much as you love Aunt Minnie, you find yourself going to visit her less and less often. Your behavior of not going to visit her is _____ by avoiding her discussion of her wayward bowels!

17. Leaving early would be another behavior that would be reinforced when you visit Aunt Minnie. The behavior is strengthened because it turns off an _____ event.

18. Turning off something _____ and giving a positive reinforcer are both important parts of the process of teaching social behaviors to children.

---

13. leaving, bowling, etc.   **14.** reinforcers   **15.** avoid

16. reinforced or strengthened   **17.** unpleasant or painful

18. painful or unpleasant

19. They both _____ behaviors.

20. Most parents will teach a child a social behavior and then reinforce him every once in a while when he does it right. However, there are other parents who somehow "forget" to use positive reinforcers. In such a home, when a child behaves himself, his mother stops nagging or scolding. In this way he too is reinforced for learning desirable social behaviors. But his mother is trained so that she _____ all of the time instead of using positive reinforcers.

21. Both positive reinforcers and punishment work in controling behavior. But the use of pain and discomfort to teach a child social behaviors means that the parent must be always on her toes, ready to punish, scold, spank, and threaten for all of the small ways in which a child can get off base. Such a household would be a rather _____ place in which to live.

22. One of the interesting things about such a household is that the family has _____ the mother to behave this way.

23. When she yells loud enough or long enough, they do what she wants them to do. In summary, it is not just children who are taught by positive reinforcers and by avoiding discomfort. It is clear that, to some extent, children teach _____ how to behave and how to run a family.

---

19. strengthen or reinforce   **20.** nags or scolds

21. unpleasant or painful **22.** trained or taught   **23.** parents

24. Another part of the process probably affects many mothers. A new mother works very hard taking care of the house and the babies. But nowadays there is very little social _____ for "being a good mother."

25. In earlier times, a grandmother or maiden aunt living in the home probably provided a good deal of _____ reinforcement for a young mother's efforts and successes. The relative usually helped with the work, too.

26. Everyone, children and adults alike, must receive a minimal amount of social reinforcement. If they do not, people are likely to feel somewhat depressed. The adult or child who receives little or no social reinforcement from anyone would eventually become a rather depressed individual. Many housewives are in this situation because they are provided with very little _____ _____. The reason for this is that children do not often reinforce mothers; and husbands are often too busy with their jobs.

27. If the husband is preoccupied with his work and not particularly interested in babies, his wife is deprived of social reinforcers and begins to feel _____.

---

24. reinforcement   25. social

26. social reinforcement   27. neglected or depressed

30

28. When a mother is not *getting* much reinforcement, she is not likely to be able to *give* many social reinforcers to either her husband or her children. Then she will train them to change behaviors by making them want to _____ the pain and discomfort of her anger.

29. By screaming and shouting, she does influence the behavior of her husband and children. Gradually, however, she must use it so often that the other people in the family may begin to avoid *her*. She then gets even fewer _____ _____.

30. As a result, she feels even more depressed and angry. In this unhappy situation the _____ trains her family to avoid her. They in turn teach her to act like a fishwife.

---

28. avoid   29. social reinforcers   30. mother

6

Accidental Training

1. This kind of training of parents by children and children by parents is largely *unplanned*. Most children do not intend to reinforce their mothers for scolding and nagging, and so on. On the other hand, most parents do not intend to _____ their children for whining or for having temper tantrums. People are usually not very much aware of what they teach each other.

2. From observations made in homes and classrooms, it seems that quite often parents accidentally _____ their children for undesirable behavior.

---

1. reinforce   2. reinforce

3. Behavior that is followed by positive reinforcers will be

   _____ .

4. One of the ironic things about most of us, as parents, is that we sometimes strengthen behaviors that we don't like and sometimes _____ behaviors that we do value in our children.

5. For example, Sally is playing with her brother. She wants the toy he is playing with. She whines and says, "Give me that toy." Her brother doesn't give her the toy, so she whines louder. Mother gets upset about the noise and tells the brother to give Sally the toy. In this situation, Sally was being reinforced for _____ .

6. The reinforcer that Sally received was the _____ .

7. The reinforcer obtained by her mother was the "turning off" of the unpleasant event of Sally's _____ .

8. Our prediction would be that in the future when things are not going the way Sally wants them to, she would

   _____ .

9. If we asked the mother why she was training her child to _____ , she would undoubtedly say that she really didn't mean to do that.

---

3. strengthened   4. weaken   5. whining   6. toy

7. whining   8. whine   9. whine

10. Probably much of the training of children is done accidentally. The fact that a child has temper tantrums or some other undesirable behavior does *not* mean that he has "bad" parents who don't love him, or who spanked too often, or who frustrated him too much. The child has temper tantrums because of poor _____ , not because of "disturbed parents."

11. Once you realize who does the reinforcing and when it occurs, it should be possible to weaken undesirable behaviors and to strengthen socially _____ behaviors. To make these changes you must first become aware of what the reinforcers are, and of when and how often you use them to strengthen behaviors.

The first step is to learn how to observe your child. This step is outlined in the next chapter.

---

10. training   **11.** acceptable or desirable

7

How to Observe
Your Child

1. Before you can change a child's behavior, you must observe it. Let's take a behavior that poses a problem for most parents, such as teaching a child to put away his clothes.

    The first step before you can change an undesirable behavior is to _____ the behavior.

2. The first step in observing your child is to decide *what it is that you are going to look at.* For a child that is untidy you might, for example, actually count the articles of clothing or toys that he leaves lying about the house. For a child with a "bad temper" you might actually _____ the number of temper tantrums he has in a day.

---

1. observe   2. count

3. As we use the words in this book, "observing" and "counting" are about the same. With something as important as your child's behavior, the task of changing it deserves your careful consideration. Teaching you to actually count the behaviors will help to make you a more careful observer. In order to count something, you must define and look at it _____.

4. Before we can teach the "messy" child some new behaviors, we first count the things that he leaves lying about the house. At first just the parents will do the counting, but later in the program they might also train the child to count his own behavior. It is best to select one time during the day and do your counting at that time. After dinner you might walk through the house and count the things lying about. When you finish counting, write down the number. In four days of counting you will have _____ of these numbers written down.

---

3. carefully or closely   4. four

5. Let's suppose that on the first night you found 19 things lying around (shoes, socks, books, empty glass, coat, etc.) and on the second night 15, on the third night 25, and on the fourth night 17. It will help if you put those numbers on a graph to give you a picture of what your child is doing. Later, when you are trying to change some of these behaviors, you will be able to see very quickly how things are changing. Here is a graph that has the data from the first two days entered. Please add in the data for the next two days. Put a dot opposite the number of things you counted above each day, then connect the dots.

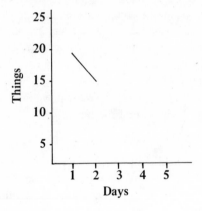

5.

6. There are a number of blank graphs included with this book. They are provided for your use in counting behaviors of *your* child. You should use one graph for each of the behaviors you wish to change. After you have counted the behaviors for several days, you are ready to plan a program with some professional person to change the behaviors. You should also *continue to count* the behaviors *during* such a program. It is important at all stages of a program for changing "undesirable behaviors" that you actually _____ the behaviors.

7. Dr. O. Lindsley proposed an interesting consequence for the "messiness" problem. Each time an article of clothing is found lying about, it is placed in the "Saturday Box" (no matter to whom it belongs). The box is not opened until Saturday. Such a consequence _____ the behaviors of leaving things lying around the house.

8. This program uses mild punishment to weaken the undesirable behavior. You should remember to also provide positive reinforcers for desirable behaviors. If the child remembers to pick up things and put them away, you could give him either a _____ or a non-_____ reinforcer.

---

6. count   7. weakens or   8. social
                     extinguishes   non-social

9. In graphing the behavior of your own child, you should
   write at the top of the graph a phrase indicating just what
   it is that you are counting. For example, a graph for a
   child with a bad temper might have a title such as
   "Number of _____ Tantrums." A child who
   is fighting too much with his brothers and sisters might
   have a graph titled "Number of Fights."

10. We can also count the times a child does a thing that we
    are training him to do. Then the graph line should go
    up instead of down as time goes on. For a child who
    won't mind, we might count the number of times he co-
    operates and use a title for his graph such as "Number of
    _____."

11. For some of the problems found in families, it is neces-
    sary not only to observe the child but the parents, too.
    For example, in some families the father seldom rein-
    forces anyone. His wife and children can take time each
    day to _____ the number of positive reinforcers
    the father gives. Or, the behavior to be changed might be
    the nagging, scolding behavior of a mother. The father
    and children in that family could count these each day.

---

9. Temper   10. Cooperations   11. count

12. On the graphs provided for your use, the vertical line at the side is left blank. Each of the marks there can stand for any number that best suits the thing you are counting. For some of the behaviors you might count, each mark might stand for one act, while for other things it might stand for ten or even twenty. Do whatever is convenient for you.

You should now begin the process of observing your child's behavior. Select one problem at a time. Count it at a regular time each _____ and for the same length of time each day.

13. When you have selected the behavior to be counted, put appropriate labels on your graph and record the number you count each day. Each graph is an accurate picture of something that your child does. As you work on a program to change a problem behavior, the graph will also give you an accurate picture of how much the behavior has actually _____.

12. day   13. changed or improved

8
Retraining

1. There are two general ideas involved in retraining your child. The first part of your program is to weaken the un-desirable behaviors; the second part, going on at the same time, is to strengthen a desirable behavior that will *compete* with the undesirable one.

   For example, if your child fights too much, you would try to weaken fighting and to _____a competing behavior such as "playing nicely" or "cooper-ating with other children."

2. Competing behaviors are those that cannot be done at the same time, such as sharing and grabbing. For each problem, then, it is up to you to think of a behavior that would replace it. For a child who won't mind, the _____ behavior might be cooperating.

---

1. strengthen   2. competing

3. For a child who cries and won't let Mother out of his sight, the competing behavior might be playing by himself. Each time such a behavior occurs you might _____ it.

4. Your task is to find ways to _____ the undesirable behavior and to strengthen the _____ behaviors.

5. Let's suppose that your son has a temper tantrum in the supermarket because he wants an ice cream cone. If you buy the cone to turn off the behavior, it is more likely that he will have_____ _____ in stores in the future.

6. One way of handling the problem is to try to cause his temper tantrums in a situation in which you will not be embarrassed by them, and then make sure that the child receives no reinforcement for having them. In other words, you _____ the temper tantrums by having them occur when there is no reinforcement for them.

7. One useful way of weakening a behavior is called a "time-out." When the child has a temper tantrum, he is told that he will have to spend five minutes in isolation (in the bathroom or basement). It is important to use the time-out procedure _____ time the child has a temper tantrum.

---

3. reinforce   4. weaken   5. temper tantrums
                     desirable

6. weaken   7. each or every

8. You must also remember to take him out of the time-out room after his _____ minutes are up. If he misbehaves in the time-out room, he should remain an extra five minutes.

9. The room you use should not be frightening to the child, like a dark closet. But it should not be reinforcing either. It should be quiet, isolated, and—above all—*very dull.* For example, there should not be toys or a _____ set in the room. Just a bare room with a light and a chair would be best.

10. When you take the child to the time-out room, you should make it a point not to be upset. Do not scold or punish on the way to the room. The reason for this is that, for some children, having parents get upset is a reinforcer for their tantrums. Be gentle, but firm! Put him in _____ *every time* he has a temper tantrum.

11. Remember that you are not going to change behavior in a single trial. It might take you a dozen temper tantrums for which you put him in time-out before you notice any change on his _____ _____ graph.

---

8. five   **9.** TV   **10.** time-out or isolation

11. problem behavior or temper tantrum

12. This means that you must *be consistent*. When a temper tantrum occurs, no matter what the situation, provide no reinforcement. Once you begin a program, if you "give in" and reinforce the undesirable behavior, it is even more powerful than when you began. Once you start a time-out program, be _____ .

13. It is also important in retraining to remember to use positive social reinforcers for behaviors that will compete with temper tantrums. For example, each time he walks through the supermarket without having a tantrum you should *praise him* for behaving himself. You might buy him the ice cream as an added _____.

14. In doing this, you are strengthening _____ behaviors, which will compete with having temper tantrums.

15. You might also announce to the rest of the family that night what a "big step" Johnny took that day, in not having his regular temper tantrums. This will provide additional positive social reinforcers for behaviors that compete with _____ _____ .

16. At the beginning of your program, try to think of the competing desirable behavior as "new"; that is, a behavior that should be reinforced very often, and as quickly

---

12. consistent   13. reinforcer   14. desirable

15. temper tantrums

as possible. You might even think up situations in which he could try out the new behaviors. In other words, you might take him to two or three stores in one morning. If he has a temper tantrum, you take him outside and make him stay in the car alone for five minutes. (You can keep an eye on him, of course.) This would be putting him in

_____-_____.

17. Your success in this kind of program depends partly on your thinking up ways in which your child can practice the "new" behaviors (and be reinforced) many, many times. Keep in mind that reinforcers must be given to him _____ times before you can expect the behavior to be strengthened very much.

18. As you begin to learn how to help your child, it is best to begin with something very simple. For example, teach your child to come to the table with clean hands before you tackle something as complex as helping him get better grades. Start with _____ behaviors first.

19. Behavior may change slowly. Do not expect the program to work until you have tried it for a number of days. For example, some children have to be placed in time-out thirty or forty times before they stop hitting their brothers and sisters. You might also give fifty to a hundred re-inforcers before the new behavior is _____ enough to replace the unwanted behavior.

---

16. time-out   17. many   18. simple

19. strengthened or strong

20. By counting, and graphing the behavior, you can *see* the changes going on—*slowly*—day by day. Do not be impatient, but remember to keep the steps small so that he always earns a great deal of reinforcement as he changes. For example, if you are reinforcing him for picking up his clothes, you might at first give him a "point" for picking up his clothes just in the living room each day. If he were successful, you would tell him how pleased you were *and* give him a point. Using a combination of social and non-social reinforcers will be more effective in strengthening the desired _____.

21. After several days of this, *if he has been successful,* you might tell him he has been doing so well that now he can earn even more points. If he cleans up both the living room and his bedroom, he will get twice as many points. After the third or fourth day, you might add another area of the house as another step. Make sure that he has been successful on one step before going on to another. And make sure that he gets a lot of _____ for each successful step.

22. When you think he is earning enough points each day, you might increase the amount of work that he has to do in order to earn the same number of points. How quickly you increase either points or work is up to the child. If your graph shows that he is no longer improving, then you should increase the amount of reinforcers *or* make the steps smaller. If behavior doesn't change, it is a bad program. When this happens, change the _____ .

---

20. behavior   **21.** reinforcement   **22.** program

23. Behavior may also stop improving because the child will tire of one type of reinforcer after a few days, such as candy. This simply means that you must change reinforcers. For example, you might try _____ or

_____ .

24. In summary, before you begin to change a defined behavior, you must first observe and_____ it.

25. Then, carefully plan the manner in which you can weaken the undesirable behavior, and the steps you can take in _____ a competing, desirable one.

26. Throughout the program you must remember to use social reinforcers along with the non-social reinforcers. Once you begin to see changes in behavior it is generally possible to decrease the non-social reinforcers. This means that you are more likely to use things like candy, points, and money at the beginning than at the _____ of the program.

27. After real improvement has occurred, you can gradually reduce the amount of toys, candy, or money being earned, but actually increase the amount of social reinforcers. In this way, _____ _____ become the most important ones for *maintaining* the new behaviors. These changes should be brought about gradually.

---

23. money or toys, or
    points for a trip, etc.

24. count or graph

25. strengthening or
    reinforcing

26. end

27. social reinforcers

28. It is also true that simply reading a book of this kind will not make you a professional child psychologist. If you have serious problems with your child, you should seek professional advice. Even with relatively minor problems you may want the advice of your pediatrician, psychologist, or school counselor. This book is not a substitute for the assistance of _____ persons.

---

28. professional

SECTION II

Changing
Undesirable Behavior

The chapters that follow provide a more detailed description of children and families with extreme problem behaviors. These families were referred because of problems severe enough to require professional help. Obviously, many of their problems were more severe than those found in the average family. For this reason, the descriptions of these families may not be helpful to all readers. However, the problems discussed here can be found in most families, but in different degrees. Because these families were kind enough to permit observers to make extensive investigations in their homes, we were able to reconstruct some of the steps that were involved in the training of these problem children.

Each of the chapters represents a different family; each chapter also outlines the "treatment program" that was used in that case. The general approach was to teach the parents the principles of social learning, and then to work in the home demonstrating how these principles could be used to help that child and that family. In all cases, the parents were trained "to do" their own treatment; and most of these parents were successful in making major changes in the behavior of their children.

9

The Child
Who Fights Too Often

1. In our society, being aggressive certainly "pays off" in
    many ways. The more aggressive adult probably sells
    more cars, makes more money, and is highly respected.
    For most adults, and children, aggressiveness is likely to
    be socially _____ by many people.

2. While in our society it may be all right for a child to hit
    once in a while, we become concerned when he is hitting
    other children very often. In this chapter, the child we
    are concerned with is the one who hits too _____.
    For example, the four year old who hits other children
    once or twice an hour is probably hitting too often.

---

1. reinforced or   2. often
   accepted

3. In planning a program for helping your child, you should begin by just observing how many times a day he actually _____ another child. Graph these amounts.

4. When a younger child is hit or pushed, he often cries. A number of research studies have shown that crying is actually a powerful reinforcer for _____ behavior.

5. If the other children give him the ball when he grabs it, or get off the bike when he pushes, and get out of the sandbox when he yells, all these consequences are _____ for aggressive behaviors.

6. In other words, the adult has only to create or permit a situation in which children cry when they are hit, or give up toys or possessions when shoved. Letting these things happen provides a situation of training children to _____.

7. There are several kinds of reinforcement for hitting, especially for young children. First, if a young child is hit, he will frequently move away and let the child who hit him have the toy, the bike, or the slide all to himself. Another kind of reinforcement is the fact that sometimes the child that is hit will _____.

8. If hitting begins to occur very often, it indicates that the parent is providing a situation in which one of the children is actually _____ to be a bully.

---

3. hits   4. hitting or aggressive   5. reinforcers

6. hit   7. cry   .   8. learning or taught

9. One boy would often hit his younger sister if she did some minor thing to annoy him. If she had a comic book that he wanted and she refused to give it to him, a hit would produce immediate results. Her giving the comic book to him was a _____ .

10. He learns to handle teasing, yelling, and other unpleasant things that siblings ordinarily do in the same manner. If they "bug" him, then he hits them and this stops the _____ .

11. The behavior "hitting" has been reinforced which means that he is likely to do it _____ .

12. Once in a while his mother may scold or spank him for hitting. While this slows him down for a few minutes, it is not very effective because he has already received much reinforcement for _____ from his siblings.

13. The problem with hitting is that "it works." The child learns that this is an effective means of changing the behavior of other people. The problem is that he uses it too _____ .

---

9. reinforcer

10. bugging, teasing, or yelling

11. again

12. hitting

13. much or often

RETRAINING

14. A time-out procedure would be one means of
weakening the hitting behavior. In using this approach,
the child is placed in time-out every time he hits.
He is also placed in time-out for all of the behaviors
that are preludes to hitting—threatening to hit,
shoving, and pushing. In this way most of the
behaviors tied in with hitting are also _____ .

15. Both the teacher and the parents are taught to use a
time-out procedure *each time* a hit occurs. In the
schoolroom if he hits other children, he is led into the
cloak room and left for five minutes. At home he
may be taken into the bathroom and left there for the
same amount of time. _____ minutes are enough
for time-out.

16. It is also necessary to give positive social reinforcers
when he behaves himself. Mothers may be so relieved
by a few minutes of peace and quiet while the children
play together that they may just want to rest. However,
in the long run, it is better to _____ him
if he plays with the other children. The behavior of
playing will compete with his fighting behavior.

---

14. weakened   15. Five   16. reinforce

17. The parent should learn to track such competing behaviors and when they occur, walk in and talk to the child about what he is doing. Being "interested" is a positive s_____ r_____ . You might even sit down and watch him for a few minutes or tell him how much you appreciate the few moments of peace and quiet.

18. While parents may very well deserve peace and quiet, they are most likely to get it if they remember to _____ it when it occurs.

19. Hitting behaviors are weakened by the use of time-out; and the competing behaviors like playing are _____ by social reinforcers.

20. It might also be a good idea in some families to have the parents strengthen behaviors that compete with hitting by using a point system. For example, each time the father or mother notice the child playing with his younger sister, they praise him and mark down a _____ in his notebook.

21. Later in the program, they might give him a point (and praise) for playing for a whole morning without _____ his younger sister.

---

17. social reinforcer   18. reinforce   19. strengthened

20. point   21. hitting

22. Even the most aggressive child can learn to drastically reduce his rate of hitting other children. This does *not* mean that he will *never* hit other children. It simply means that he will hit other people much less than he did. The idea is to _____ the frequency of aggressive behavior, not to completely remove it.

23. When these reductions occur, most mothers report that they feel differently about the child now that he is behaving himself. It is surprising how many mothers get driven to actually hating their children. Because the behavior of some children is so unpleasant to parents, it is easy to see how this can happen. But as behavior improves, these feelings also _____ .

---

22. lower, reduce, or lessen

23. change or improve

10

The
"I Don't Want to" Child

1. There are no children who mind all the time. However, there are some children who, as they get older, seem to have a one-word vocabulary: "No." Negativistic is a term for children who refuse to obey, who say "no" all the time. Children of any age can be _____.

2. "Eat your potatoes, Johnny." As Mother says this, Johnny pushes his plate further away. This parent has to ask five or six times before the child will even start. He also has to be asked to hang up his coat five or six times before he responds. By not hanging up his coat, he can control his mother's attention for five or ten minutes. This _____ him for being negativistic.

---

1. negativistic   2. reinforces

3. In making your observations, you could count either the number of times Johnny minds when asked to do something, or you could _____ the number of times he refuses to cooperate.

4. Counting either the undesirable behavior or the competing _____ behavior will give you about the same information.

5. Some adults, too, have discovered that negativism pays off. When a group of people are sitting around talking, one sure way to control the attention of members of the group is to begin to disagree with what everyone else is saying. When you disagree, they generally stop talking to each other and talk to _____.

6. For these adults, and for many children, negativism is one way they can produce a predictable reaction from their environment. The family has probably trained such a child by really paying attention to him only when he refused to _____.

7. When a child says "No," some parents try to bribe him into cooperating. The bribe, of course, even further _____ the negativism.

---

3. count   4. desirable   5. you

6. obey, cooperate,   7. strengthens or reinforces
   or agree

8. Some children simply *ignore* the requests made by parents. In either case, the parent has probably not been reinforcing the child for *cooperating*. Cooperation involves a set of behaviors that would _____ with negativism.

9. If, for example, there were no reinforcement for minding, this desirable behavior would eventually be _____.

10. Even adults have to be reinforced occasionally for co-operating. Adults have all kinds of rules to insure that reinforcement occurs when someone cooperates. For example, you say "_____ _____" when someone opens a door for you.

RETRAINING

11. A program for working with negativism would have to include a way of weakening the negativistic behaviors. If the child shouts "No," it should be ignored. The effect of ignoring this negativism would be to _____ it.

12. You could actually put the child into a time-out room each time he refuses to cooperate, but it is our guess that such a program would be stormy and take a rather long time. We can speed this up by concentrating on strengthening the competing _____ of cooperating.

---

8. compete   9. weakened   10. Thank you

11. weaken   12. behavior

13. You might set up practice situations, choosing those in which he usually cooperates. Make one of these requests and when he _____, reinforce him.

14. Again, you would want to use both social and non-social reinforcers (such as points or treats). These reinforcers should be given _____ time and given immediately for each cooperative behavior.

15. You would keep the steps "small" by first beginning with requests he generally obeys and working up to situations in which he almost never cooperates. For example, you might begin by asking him to go across the room and pick up a magazine and bring it to you. All one child did when we suggested that he do this was to glance toward the magazine. The reinforcers were, "Good, you at least looked at it," and one M&M candy. The first response to be _____ in teaching this boy to cooperate was "looking."

16. At the next request he took one step toward the magazine, and again received a social reinforcer and another M&M (which he shared with his brother. Sometimes it helps to let the other children earn treats by playing the games, too). Later still, he received one M&M for each step he took toward the magazine. The size, or kind, of steps that you set up in these programs depends on the child. His _____ tells you what the step should be.

---

13. obeys or cooperates   **14.** each or every

15. strengthened or rein-   **16.** behavior
      forced

17. Gradually introduce situations in which the child is usually negativistic. You might tell him that you appreciate the fact that he is changing his behavior. If you see that the program is not working, then you should either make the steps _____ or give more reinforcers.

18. You might also try a new _____.
    After several days, a child will sometimes tire of the same reinforcer, and it becomes necessary to introduce a new one.

19. After discussing it with the child, you might decide that he could earn 100 points for a special weekend trip with his father. He would earn these points one at a time on each occasion that he _____ with a request.

---

17. smaller   **18.** reinforcer   **19.** cooperated

11

The Overly Active, Noisy Child

1. The program that follows was written for parents who had trained their child to be "overactive." These parents were good examples of how easy it is to accidentally reinforce children for _____ behavior and to fail to reinforce them for _____ behavior.

2. Ray, a noisy, overactive child, was constantly on the move. He moved about his house and his classroom at such a rate that it was unpleasant to have him around. It is very hard not to pay attention to an _____ child.

---

1. undesirable,   2. overactive
   desirable

3. To count these behaviors, you might put down a mark for each loud, noisy event. You might also mark running or moving around very fast. Being noisy and being very active are not necessarily the same thing; therefore, you should perhaps put them on different _____.

4. When mothers are busy housecleaning, ironing, fixing dinner, and so on, they don't wish to be disturbed by children's shouting or misbehaving. A fast-moving, noisy child's behavior is likely to be especially _____.

5. No matter how busy she is, the overactive child is some-one to whom the mother must pay _____.

6. Ray's mother hurried into the room when she heard her two boys getting "wound up" and yelled at them to "slow down." After she threatened them, the children were quiet. The fact that they were now quiet reinforced the mother for _____ at the children.

7. The boys began to play again. Both of them were pushing model cars across the room. One boy pushed his car a little harder and it bumped into the wall. When Ray pushed his car hard, the behavior was _____ by his brother's giggling.

---

3. graphs or charts   4. unpleasant or   5. attention
                                disturbing

6. yelling   7. reinforced

8. Ray then pushed his car very hard. It rocketed across the room and slammed into a chair. His brother laughed, picked up his own car and pushed it into a table. Both of them laughed very loudly. At this point, both boys were _____ each other for making noise.

9. They now began to run about the house, chasing each other, yelling, and giggling as they ran. The two boys were reinforcing each other for being noisy and for being extremely active. In desperation, Mother finally said, "Your father will spank you when he gets home." As stated earlier, to use positive or negative reinforcers most effectively, they should be provided _____ after the behavior occurs.

10. Since this negative result (spanking) would come several hours after the undesirable behavior, we would not expect it to have much long-term effect in _____ the behaviors.

11. Soon the boys started running and shouting again. The fact that they were quiet even for a short while, however, did _____ the mother's threatening them.

12. Because her threatening did have some temporary effect upon the children's behavior, the mother will continue threatening her children. She was reinforced for threatening and yelling because it produced a short-term _____ in her children's behavior.

---

8. reinforcing   9. immediately   10. weakening

11. reinforce   12. effect or improvement

13. After a time, the children have taught their mother to scold and nag. The mother comes to think of the children as being "bad" and "always getting into things." At this point she is so well trained that she is unpleasant to them even when they behave in _____ ways.

14. Our observations suggest that active boys are most likely to *start* making noise and running about when they have been deprived of social reinforcers. The noise and running become one of the few means available for getting any attention at all. In a sense they force people to _____ them for being noisy.

15. In a family that doesn't react very much, running about and making noise are ways of forcing the environment to provide _____ _____.

16. Sometimes the children have to keep getting louder and louder to get a reaction. The reaction comes only when they are very noisy. This process of working harder for the same amount of reinforcement will teach the children to be even more _____.

---

13. desirable   14. reinforce   15. social reinforcement

16. noisy

RETRAINING

17. Most parents in this type of family tend to no longer notice that there are many times when the overactive child slows down, or is quiet. If they do not notice, of course, they cannot _____ him for these behaviors when they do occur.

18. During the first few days of a retraining program, the parents might count the number of times they reinforce the child for doing something quietly. Most likely they do not reinforce him for such behaviors; so these behaviors will not be _____.

19. Earlier we described how to get rid of unacceptable behavior by reinforcing behavior that competes with it. Therefore, Ray's mother should reinforce him for behavior that cannot occur at the same time as noisy and _____ behavior.

20. To strengthen desirable behaviors, the mother might begin by asking the child to color some pictures. If he does, she *must* take a few seconds to look at what he is coloring and to show some interest in what he is doing. Doing this is reinforcing behaviors that _____ with being noisy and disturbing.

---

17. reinforce

18. strengthened

19. undesirable or overactive

20. compete

21. It is up to each parent to think of situations like this that would help her child practice sitting still and being quiet. Perhaps he sits still when you read to him or talk to him. If this is so, you might _____ to him several times a day for brief periods.

22. If the graph shows that after a few days of the program, he is not slowing down, Ray's parents might decide to use the point system. Now, in addition to praise, put a point in his notebook each time he can sit quietly for one minute. Gradually, the number of minutes of quiet play necessary to earn a point would be _____.

23. Much later in the program he might have to play quietly for as long as an hour in order to earn his point. Let's say that he has been working for five minutes and earning points (and praise) consistently. Suppose that now you require that he sit quietly for ten minutes to earn a point. If your graph shows that he is not earning many points then you must make your step increase *smaller*. For example, increase it to _____ minutes rather than ten.

24. Parents should expect slow changes, however, during the first few days. If he is an extremely active child, you may wish to begin by having him sit and color in the same room where you are working. This makes it possible for you to reinforce him very frequently. At first, such a child might require _____ reinforcers.

---

21. read or talk   **22.** increased   **23.** 6, 7, or 8

24. many

25. Gradually, as he is able to play quietly for long periods of time in the same room with you, then he might play in a room next to the one you are in. When he makes that shift, you might have to again use very small steps. For example, when he is in a room by himself he might get a point for every _____ minutes that he plays by himself even though when he is in the same room with you he can play quietly for half an hour.

26. You might announce to your husband each night at dinner with the child present the number of points he earned and mention how pleased you are with the fact that he sits quietly for even a little while during the day. In the evening and on weekends, the _____ should participate in the practice sessions with him.

27. Children also tend to reinforce each other for loud, rough play. For this reason, the parents might also plan a program to prevent brothers and sisters from _____ each other's overactive, noisy behavior.

28. This can be done by using a time-out. When the other children are involved with the problem child in being overly active and noisy, they are *all* given a "time-out" in _____ rooms.

---

25. five   26. father   27. reinforcing

28. separate

29. During the time-out period, the children cannot receive any positive reinforcement from _____ _____.

30. If there is no reinforcement for being noisy, then the noisy behaviors should _____.

31. Every time the children become too noisy, quickly take them to their respective rooms for a full _____ minutes. After a few days, the children will learn that they are not reinforced for being noisy.

32. In this household, now, the only way to get the father's or mother's attention is by playing _____ and being reasonably "good" children.

---

29. each other or   **30.** weaken   **31.** five
any one

32. quietly

12

The Dependent Child

1. Earlier in this discussion, it was noted that sometimes
    parents accidentally _____ children
    when they behave in undesirable ways.

2. We believe that often parents find themselves teaching
    their child to be helpless and infantile. An infant must
    be dependent upon his environment because he is help-
    less. He cannot feed himself. As he grows he becomes
    increasingly able to take care of himself. He learns to
    crawl and later to walk. He learns to talk and dress him-
    self. However, some parents continue to reinforce their
    child for being _____ .

---

1. reinforce   2. helpless or dependent

3. He becomes so helpless that he depends upon the parents to do many things he could do himself. Imagine a seven-year-old child who cannot dress himself. When he asks his mother to tie his shoe for him, she does. This reinforces him for being helpless or _____ . As an alternative, she could teach him to tie his own shoe.

4. Another form of dependent behavior involves always being "close" to mother. If the mother is in the kitchen, the child is in the kitchen. The _____ child may even sleep with his parents.

5. If the mother is trying to talk to friends, this child is crawling over her lap, whining, and asking for things. The _____ child has great difficulty in sharing the social reinforcers given out by the parent.

6. Dependent people behave in such a way as to obtain social reinforcement—attention, sympathy, help, and affection. As grownups, these are the people who are always calling someone on the telephone and asking for advice or help. Such a person might call a half dozen people in one day. The dependent child or adult seems to require a great deal of _____ reinforcement.

---

3. dependent   **4.** dependent   **5.** dependent

6. social

7. For example, the dependent child would prefer to stay in the house with his parents than to go outside and play with other children. There are also dependent adults who must live with their parents or have their parents close by. It is clear that people do not just "grow out" of being _____.

8. The dependent person tends to use a special approach in "earning" his reinforcers. His general technique is to behave as if he is "helpless," and to get people to _____ him for it.

9. In observing and counting dependent behaviors in your child, you might count things such as the number of requests for help or the number of minutes he spends playing by himself or with other children. You should select a regular period during the day when you collect these data and do this for at least three or _____ days before you begin to change any behavior.

10. It is hard to say just why some parents reinforce dependent behavior. Some reinforce the child for being helpless because at an earlier time the child had a serious illness. When sick in bed, all of us are strongly reinforced for being _____. Sometimes a mother will simply forget to stop "nursing" a child.

---

7. dependent   8. reinforce   9. four

10. helpless or dependent

11. Other parents simply want to make life as pleasant as possible for their child and tend to do everything for him. In that case, too much sympathy results in the child's being reinforced for _____ behaviors.

12. There are also parents who seem to teach their children to depend upon them in order to fill a need in their own lives. These people are terribly lonely and, in a sense, are actually training someone to "lean" on them. Whatever the reason, the training process is the same. All of these parents reinforce the child for being _____.

13. If Diane's mother left to go into the next room, the three-year-old would begin to cry. The mother would then turn around, go back and pick her up. The reinforcement for the crying behavior was being _____ _____.

14. This kind of training went on hundreds of times a day! This mother could literally not be out of Diane's sight. In such a situation, again, we have a mother who is training her child to be _____, and the result of this training is to make both the mother and child miserable. It is odd, but the fact is that quite often we teach other people to behave in such a way as to injure ourselves.

---

11. helpless or dependent

12. dependent or helpless

13. picked up

14. dependent

15. Billy's mother works and has to leave home before it is time for him to go to school. Billy is slow. She has to dress him. She is forced to _____ him for being helpless. Even though he's a third-grader, he eats so slowly that she must feed him in the morning.

16. She doesn't want him to help her around the house because he always makes a mess. He can't even set the table without dropping something on the floor. After dinner she plays a game with him, reads to him, and puts him to bed. This child lives in a world where he has to do very little in order to be paid off. He is dressed, fed, and entertained by one person. The way his reinforcers are earned almost guarantees that he will continue to be_____.

17. It is not surprising that when he faces some other environment where he must respond appropriately in order to be positively reinforced, he does not do well. When he is first taken to school, he is frightened. The fear is real. Being left with a baby sitter can also make him _____.

18. Anything that separates this dependent child from his mother can produce deep _____.

---

15. reinforce   **16.** dependent   **17.** afraid or frightened

18. fear

RETRAINING

19. After a few days of observing, you should have a fair idea of how often the behavior occurs and where and when it is being reinforced. You must now begin to practice (if you are the main reinforcer) ignoring the _____ behavior when it occurs. You might have to educate your spouse or baby sitter to follow the program, too.

20. Not reinforcing these behaviors will eventually _____ them. However, this would mean that a great many people are now giving him less reinforcers than he usually gets. This sudden shift could make him rather unhappy.

21. Therefore, when you begin the program to weaken the dependent behaviors, you should also provide extra social reinforcers. Give positive reinforcers for behaviors that will _____ with the dependent behaviors. These would be behaviors showing that he is helping himself and able to be independent.

22. For example, if getting dressed is a problem, you might reinforce him for dressing himself. Here, too, you would reinforce him at first for very small _____ in dressing himself.

---

19. dependent   20. weaken   21. compete

22. steps

23. In the early stages of training him to be independent, reinforcement should be given _____ and given immediately whenever one of these behaviors occurs. One of your tasks will be thinking of situations in which he can practice the new behaviors.

24. The first day, it might be reinforcement for just finding his shoes, then later for putting them on, then for finding the rest of his clothes. You are training him _____ _____ _____ to be more independent.

25. Eventually, you will also want to _____ him for playing with other children or being with the baby sitter. You are training him to be *away from mother.*

26. It is particularly important to teach him that he can receive reinforcement from many persons and not just his _____ . Teaching him that he can get reinforcement from other children would be a big step in this direction.

27. It is important to tell the child frequently how pleased you are with the fact that he is growing up and learning to be independent. You might make regular announcements to the rest of the family to the effect that today Billy dressed himself, or he played outside by himself, or he didn't cry once. Not only is this reinforcing for the child, but it also reminds the family that they can assist in the program. Not just the parents, but the whole _____ can participate in these programs.

---

23. often or frequently   **24.** step by step   **25.** reinforce

26. mother   **27.** family

13

The Frightened Child

1. Fear is not necessarily a bad thing. It is important, for example, that a child learn to be somewhat _____ of the cars going by on the street.

2. It is also probably good for every young child to be somewhat _____ of fires and bodies of water.

3. Most people are afraid of some things. What we are concerned about here is the child who shows many fears or who has such extreme fear that he cannot learn.

   There are *several* ways of learning to be afraid. One way is to watch other people who are afraid. If there is a storm, and children see that their mother is afraid, then they will probably be _____ of storms.

---

1. afraid   2. afraid   3. afraid

4. If a young girl sees her grandmother shriek and jump on a chair in obvious fright when a mouse runs across the room, it is very likely that the girl will learn to fear _____ .

5. If a child (or adult) lives with people who constantly talk about being afraid of the dark and talk about the horrible things that can happen in the dark, then it becomes very likely that the child will learn to be afraid of the dark. If a family talks continually about how strangers can hurt you, or how they kidnap children, eventually a child in such a family will learn to be frightened when around _____ .

6. A parent who was frightened and tense when near water or out in the woods would almost certainly teach his child to be afraid in these situations. A number of research studies have shown that mothers who have many fears have children who have many of the same _____ .

7. Keep in mind that most of us learn to stop being afraid of many of these things. Fear, then, is a behavior that is _____ , and the child can be trained in such a way as to increase or decrease his fear.

---

4. mice   5. strangers   6. fears

7. learned

8. There is another important way of learning fears. A child can be extremely fearful, even though none of his family have shown fear when around him. Such a fear often appears when a young child is separated from his parents. Because the fear is triggered when the child is being separated from his parents, it is called "separation fear." The child who is frightened when left with the baby sitter may be showing _____ fear.

9. Some children do not learn how to obtain social reinforcers from other children or from grownups other than their parents. The only people in the world that function as reinforcers for such a child are his

_____ .

10. Every time his mother wishes to go to a movie, leave the child with a baby sitter, or take him to Sunday School, the child becomes _____ .

11. Such a child is probably not being mean or naughty. He is genuinely afraid because he has not yet learned that people other than _____ can be reinforcing.

12. A young child may not have learned that the behavior of other children is reinforcing. In other words, if you suddenly place him alone with a room full of children, he may be in a situation where he is actually receiving no positive _____ at all.

---

8. separation   9. parents   10. afraid or
                                   frightened

11. mother or parents   12. reinforcement

13. Children, animals, and adults become very emotional when their supply of reinforcers is stopped. The adult could probably tell you that he feels sad, lonely, tense, or perhaps homesick when off alone on a trip. Feeling upset when your supply of social reinforcers is not available is uncomfortable, but is perfectly normal. Being uncomfortable when social reinforcers are not available is a feeling children get, and so do most

_____ .

14. Johnny's mother might try to stop his crying on the first day at school by giving him sympathy and comfort. Attention and comforting are powerful _____ reinforcers to Johnny.

15. If he stops crying when she comforts him, then she is reinforced for "mothering him." Now *she* is being reinforced for giving him _____ when he cries. And the child is getting a positive social reinforcer for crying.

16. As long as Johnny is positively reinforced for crying when he is afraid, he will _____ and he will show this behavior whenever he is separated from his mother.

17. In fact, if this is repeated day after day, Johnny will probably be increasingly afraid to go to _____ .

---

13. adults   14. social   15. comfort or attention

16. cry   17. school

18. What you will observe and count depends on what kind of fear your child displays. It could be the number of times during the day that he comes and tells you about frightening things. It could also be the number of times during the day that he objects to your leaving him. The important thing is to determine the number of times each _____ that he is afraid.

RETRAINING

19. To change fears you must do more than just wait until the child grows older. You must specifically *train* him *not to be afraid*. Several studies show that just arguing with a child, or trying to "talk him out of it" will not work very well. What seems to be required is to teach the child (or adult) some behaviors he can use whenever he finds himself in the situation that causes _____ .

20. The problem is to find some way of _____ him not to be afraid.

21. For example, in working with adults who are afraid to give public speeches, they are first carefully trained to *relax* all of the muscles in their body. Then they are trained to _____ their muscles while speaking to an imaginary audience.

22. The idea is that you cannot do two competing things at the same time. You can't be relaxed and _____ at the same time.

---

18. day   **19.** fear   **20.** teaching or training

21. relax   **22.** afraid or tense

23. Because of this training, when these people are asked to give a speech to a real audience, they react with _____ muscles rather than with _____.

24. The same idea is used to teach infants not to be afraid of the water while in the bathtub. The child is given M&M candies for each few seconds that he sits in the water without crying. You can't very well _____ candy and _____ at the same time.

25. Later the child is given plastic toys to play with. He is reinforced with the M&M candies for _____ with the toys while he sits in the water. You cannot play with toys and cry at the same time (at least it is an unlikely combination).

26. As a first step, you might put only a small amount of water in the tub. Gradually, as the fear lessens, you can raise the _____ level. Your child's behavior determines how much the steps can be increased.

27. Some children are afraid of their potty chair. In teaching behaviors that compete with such fears, you might begin by having him sit fully dressed on the _____ _____ for just a few seconds.

---

23. relaxed,   24. eat,   25. playing
    fear or tension   cry

26. water   27. potty chair

86

28. Gradually you increase the size of the steps until he can
sit there for perhaps 30 seconds *with his clothes on.* In
addition to candy, and praise, you might now read part of
a story to him as long as he sits there without _____ .

29. After a few trials he must sit there for a few seconds with
his trousers down and listen to the story without crying.
The competing behavior being reinforced here is
_____ to the story.

30. If the fear is related to fears about separation, retraining
may be somewhat more complicated. For such a child
you might have to first teach him that there are other
people in the world besides the mother who can provide
him with positive _____ _____ .

31. The idea is to teach him that the baby sitter, the teacher,
and other children can be _____ .

32. You might begin by practicing with him at home. For
example, you might say, "I'm going to the basement to
start the laundry. Goodbye, see you soon." Give him a
point (and praise) if he can say goodbye without

_____ .

---

28. crying   **29.** listening   **30.** social reinforcers

31. reinforcers   **32.** crying

33. You might then use practice sessions in which his grand-mother or a neighbor is present while you are saying goodbye to him. The other adult should be someone the child knows rather well. You could place the child in her lap, say goodbye and walk out the door. If the child does not cry she immediately _____ him with praise and candy and the mother returns after just a few moments.

34. The steps involved here are based on the number of minutes the mother stays outside the door. After ten or twenty such practice sessions on the first morning, the mother might wait outside the door for ten minutes before she returns. On each trial, it is not the mother but the other _____ who gives the immediate reinforcer for not crying.

35. If the child begins crying while the mother stands outside, she should wait until the crying stops before returning. If she returns when he cries, she is again _____ him for crying.

36. You might then practice with your best baby sitter. Have her give him points or other rewards as soon as his crying slows down after you leave. Then she can give him points when he has not been crying for a minute, then five minutes, etc. She might give him points for playing a game with her. He cannot (very well) play a game and _____.

---

33. reinforces   **34.** adult or person   **35.** reinforcing

36. cry

37. When Johnny, who was extremely fearful, started school, it was necessary to have his mother sit in the classroom and _____ him each time he *stopped* clutching her sleeve.

38. Eventually, Johnny's mother was able to reinforce him (with candy, and praise) for _____ with other children in the nursery school.

39. The mother might also have other children come to the home and provide a great deal of reinforcers for playing together for even brief periods of time. The child would thus learn that _____ are reinforcing.

40. When he played, the children gave him social reinforcers. He learned in the process that people other than just _____ could provide reinforcers for him.

41. In school, he was reinforced by the teacher and by the other children for playing. As he became more skillful in getting along in the nursery school, these skills competed with the occurrence of _____.

---

37. reinforce   38. playing   39. children

40. mother or parents   41. fear

14

The Withdrawn Child

1. The withdrawn or non-responsive child is one who seems to spend as little time as possible with other people. If someone talks to him, this child is likely to say only one or two words in reply. He almost never looks at people when they speak to him. He seldom smiles. This boy doesn't reinforce other _____ when they try to talk with him.

2. Most of us stop talking to someone who never replies, never looks at us, and never looks interested in what we are saying. People must be _____, even for talking to their own children or spouses.

---

1. people   2. reinforced

3. Jerry's mother comes into the room where he is playing and says, "Hi, what are you doing?" The boy does not look up. He does not act pleased with her question. He mumbles, "Playing army." None of these reactions from the boy would be positive reinforcers for his mother's

   _____.

4. If this happened between Jerry and his parents several hundred times, then we would expect his parents to stop _____ to him.

5. At this point we have a situation in which a child has taught his own parents to let him alone. Even if he is in a room with a large number of people, such a child is alone. He has _____ all of them to "stay away."

6. Some children who are withdrawn and nonresponsive seem to find toys or books to be more reinforcing than

   _____.

7. For such a child, playing with toy soldiers is more reinforcing than _____ to parents.

8. There are adults, too, who find that books, stamps, or hobbies offer more reinforcers than _____ do.

---

3. behavior or talking   4. talking   5. taught

6. people   7. talking   8. people

9. There are probably a number of ways to teach a child that people are not interesting reinforcers. If the parents frequently use punishment in teaching their children, the child may tend to avoid people. Staying away from people is reinforcement for the _____ child because it turns off painful events.

10. The form of punishment some parents apply is not spanking or slapping; it is rather a kind of "sarcasm." The parents' frown or sarcastic comment is a constant reminder to the child that he is bad, or stupid, or worthless. The punishment is constant. This kind of punishment is probably at least as painful as a _____ .

11. In such a family, staying away from people would be one way of turning off the painful situation. This is another way of saying that "withdrawing" may be _____ for some children.

12. In observing the behavior of this child, you might decide to count the number of minutes that he spends playing or _____ with other people.

---

9. withdrawn   10. spanking or slap   11. reinforcing

12. talking

RETRAINING

13. One of the first things we must teach Jerry is that his parents *are reinforcers*. One way of doing this is to associate his parents with things that are already powerful reinforcers for him. Make a list of things that are powerful reinforcers for your child.

1. _____ 4. _____
2. _____ 5. _____
3. _____ 6. _____

14. You might observe to see how often you use painful events and punishment to control his behavior. If you do use it often, your first step should be to decrease the amount of punishment and to increase the amount of social _____ you give him.

15. In the early part of the program, a point system can be used so that the child earns one of these non-social reinforcers. For example, when the child earns 100 points, he might be taken to a restaurant where he gets one of his favorite desserts. Every few days you might change the reinforcer he is earning with his _____.

16. Always, as the child earns a point, the parent also gives a social reinforcer. For example, "That was very good, and you just earned a point, too. You are getting to be quite a talker." When using the point system *always* accompany a point with a _____ _____.

---

13. candy, ice cream,   14. reinforcement   15. points
money, toys, watch
TV, go on rides, etc.

16. social reinforcer

17. Some parents have to learn to listen. Jerry's parents are encouraged to give points and social reinforcers when he even "looks as if he wants to talk." When this happens, they stop what they are doing and _____ to him.

18. You also have to "practice" noticing what it is that your child does. You will be surprised to find that even the most withdrawn and shy child actually makes many efforts to approach other _____.

19. However, when he does try to get people interested in him, he is cautious and unskilled and they usually just _____ him.

20. If he says anything to you, you must be very sure that you *listen* to what he says. Your _____ is a reinforcer for his talking. Of course, you might also give him a point.

21. As Jerry's mother, you are out of the habit of listening to him. So you might pick a certain time of day at first when you are going to practice this. For example, at meal times you will try to ask Jerry a few questions and _____ to his replies.

22. You can help him learn that this chatting is pleasant by not letting other members of the family interrupt when Jerry is _____.

---

17. listen   18. people   19. ignore

20. listening   21. listen   22. talking

23. Also, it would help if you did not let them change the subject Jerry is talking about. If people changed the subject after each comment that you made, you would probably not find this _____.

24. As you teach him to be less shy and withdrawn at home, Jerry will try out his new behaviors in other places. If he tries these things a few times, it is very likely that other people will also reinforce him. However, it is up to you people, his family, to _____ the process.

---

23. reinforcing   **24.** begin or start

BEHAVIOR GRAPH

Daily Observations of _____ 's _____

(name)　　　　　　　　　　　(behavior)

Number of times counted

Days

DATE	POINTS	DATE	POINTS	DATE	POINTS

BEHAVIOR GRAPH

Daily Observations of _____ 's _____

                            (name)   (behavior)

Number of times counted

Days

DATE	POINTS	DATE	POINTS	DATE	POINTS

BEHAVIOR GRAPH

Daily Observations of _____ 's _____

(name)   (behavior)

Number of times counted

Days

DATE	POINTS	DATE	POINTS	DATE	POINTS